Winging It

By Don Aker

Series Literacy Consultant
Dr Ros Fisher

Pearson Education Limited
Edinburgh Gate
Harlow
Essex CM20 2JE
England

www.longman.co.uk

ISBN 0 582 84150 X

Colour reproduction by Colourscan, Singapore
Printed and bound in China by Leo Paper Products Ltd.

The Publisher's policy is to use paper manufactured from sustainable forests.

10 9 8 7 6 5 4 3

The following people from **DK** have
contributed to the development of this product:

Art Director Rachael Foster

Martin Wilson **Managing Art Editor**	**Managing Editor** Marie Greenwood
Clair Watson **Design**	**Editorial** Selina Wood
Brenda Clynch **Picture Research**	**Production** Rosalind Holmes
Richard Czapnik, Andy Smith **Cover Design**	**DTP** David McDonald

Consultant David Burnie

Dorling Kindersley would like to thank: Peter Bull for illustration; Ed Merritt for cartography; Rose Horridge, Hayley Smith and Gemma Woodward in the DK Picture Library; Penny Smith for editorial assistance; Johnny Pau for additional cover design work.

Picture Credits: Ardea London Ltd: 34tl; Jean-Paul Ferrero 24br; Clem Haagner 17b, 18crb; George Reszeter 13bl. Corbis: Macduff Everton 38bl; Philip Marazzi/Papilio 26b; Roger Tidman 35; Stuart Westmorland 19clb. DK Images: Natural History Museum 7cr, 10tl, 13tr, 13cra, 13crb, 13br, 32r, 33cr, 33b; © Peabody Museum of Natural History, Yale University. All Rights Reserved 6b. FLPA - Images of nature: 32bl; H.D. Brandt 22br; Bill Coster 37cra; N. Dennis 23b; T & P Gardner 11b, 24tl; A. Hamblin 16bl; David Hosking 37crb; D. Maslowski 19cra; Minden Pictures 16br, 27bc, 31crb, 37tr, 37br; Fritz Polking 20t; Len Robinson 11tr; W. Rohdich 34br; Roger Tidman 36-37b; Terry Whittacker 16cl; Roger Wilmshurst 22tl; Winfried Wisniewski 31t. Nature Picture Library Ltd: Niall Benvie 29t;Bristol City Museum 38tl; Ingo Arndt 4cl; Pete Oxford 32tl; Mike Wilkes 28br. The Natural History Museum, London: 7tl, 8. N.H.P.A.: Vicente Garcia Canseco 23tr; Stephen Dalton 4b; Stephen Krasemann 9t, 27tr; Mike Lane 26tl; Julie Meech 25tr; David Middleton 19cla, 37cr; Kevin Schafer 5t; Dave Watts 14b. Oxford Scientific Films: Gary & Terry Andrewartha/Sal 16cr; Robert Tyrrell 4tl. Science Photo Library: Sid Baht 30b; George D.Lepp 27br. Dave Watts: 31cb. Woodfall Wild Images: Steve Austin 18cra. Jacket: Ardea London Ltd: Peter Steyn front t. Getty Images: Joseph Van Os front b. Nature Picture Library Ltd: Bristol City Museum back.

All other images: DK Dorling Kindersley © 2004. For further information see www.dkimages.com
Dorling Kindersley Ltd., 80 Strand, London WC2R ORL

Contents

How Adaptation Works

Cuban bee hummingbird

rhea

A tiny hummingbird hovers and sips from a flower, its bright feathers shimmering. Thousands of miles away, a dull-brown rhea strides through tall grass searching for seeds. Meanwhile, on the other side of the world, a barn owl flaps through the dark night, listening for prey.

Birds come in an amazing variety of shapes and sizes. They live all over the world, from the freezing Antarctic to parched deserts and steamy rainforests. Most birds fly, though a few cannot. Many hop, run or walk and some dive and swim. Most birds are active during the day. Others hunt and feed at night, and sleep during the day.

barn owl

Different types of birds do not look the same and they do not act the same way. The many differences among birds are the result of **adaptations**.

An adaptation is something that makes it easier for a living thing to survive in its environment, or habitat. An adaptation may be a change in a body part or in behaviour. Adaptations develop over long periods of time.

Emperor penguins have adapted to survive in an extremely cold habitat.

A bird must find food and water, protect itself from weather extremes and avoid being eaten if it is to survive. In every **species**, or type, of bird, some individuals are better than others at surviving. These particular birds tend to live longest and reproduce successfully.

When these birds have babies, the parents pass their characteristics on to the next generation. The birds that do not adapt well die out. Over many generations, each species becomes better adapted to its habitat through this process of **natural selection**.

How Early Birds Developed

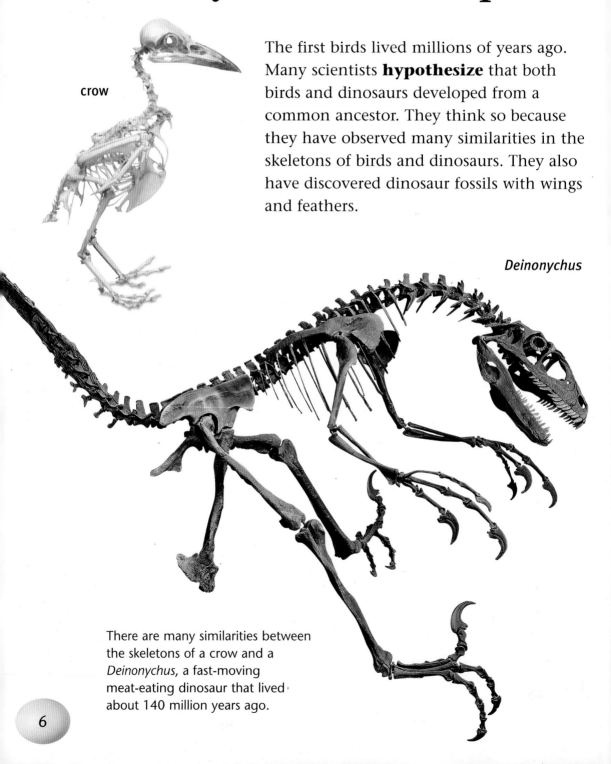

crow

The first birds lived millions of years ago. Many scientists **hypothesize** that both birds and dinosaurs developed from a common ancestor. They think so because they have observed many similarities in the skeletons of birds and dinosaurs. They also have discovered dinosaur fossils with wings and feathers.

Deinonychus

There are many similarities between the skeletons of a crow and a *Deinonychus*, a fast-moving meat-eating dinosaur that lived about 140 million years ago.

6

long feathers

The first known bird, *Archaeopteryx*, was discovered in central Europe. It was about the size of a crow.

wing of a roller bird

The Ability to Fly

It is not known how birds' ancestors first began to fly. One possibility is that they had **scales**, and lived high in trees, gliding from branch to branch.

An animal with long scales would have been able to glide further than an animal with short scales. Longer scales would have produced more drag, or air resistance, and would have slowed an animal's fall as it glided.

Being able to glide further would have helped the longer-scaled animals avoid **predators** on the ground. They would have been more likely to survive and pass on their characteristics to their **descendants**. Over many generations, the long scales may have improved until they resembled feathers.

Why birds can fly

Two features of birds that make it possible for birds to fly are their wing structure and light bones. The wing is strong and flexible. Different groups of feathers help the bird lift off and stay in flight. The bones of birds are very light and often hollow. This is important because heavy bones would make it impossible to fly.

The Role of Fluffy Feathers

Birds may have developed in a different way. Millions of years ago, dinosaur-like animals ran along the ground on their hind legs. They needed warm muscles to run quickly. Fluffy feathers could have developed as **insulation** to keep the muscles warm.

If this idea is accurate, then these first feathers probably helped the animals to balance and to jump higher, too. As a result they could hunt more successfully, which improved their chances of survival. Feathers would have improved slowly over time, until eventually early birds could fly.

insulating fluff

A fossil of a young *Dromaeosaurus,* found in China, with insulating fluff

Canada geese fly to warmer climates in the autumn to escape northern winters.

The Benefits of Flying

How did the ability to fly change the future of the earliest birds? Like all successful animal **adaptations**, it was a way of improving chances of survival.

Flying helps birds get to distant food sources, and is a very good way of escaping danger. It also enables birds to migrate from a cold place to a warmer one.

Each spring, Canada geese fly to Canada and Alaska to breed. In the autumn they fly south to the warmer climates of Mexico and the southern United States.

Alaska

Canada

United States

Mexico

Map Key

↑ Spring migration

↓ Autumn migration

Structural Adaptations

Clearly, flying was a successful adaptation but it meant that other **adaptations** were also necessary. Birds had to develop a way to hold objects and prey. Over time they developed specialized bills and feet.

Birds also had to become lighter so they developed bones with air spaces. Ancient bird-dinosaurs had teeth, but birds do not have them today. Jaws with teeth are heavy. Now birds have gizzards instead, which are special muscles in their stomach that grind food. They also have organs called crops at the base of the neck where food is stored and prepared for digestion. Changes like these in an animal's body are called **structural adaptations.**

This cross-section of a bird's bone shows large hollow pockets. These air spaces are adaptations that make bird bones light, but strong.

anatomy of a bird

lungs

crop

bill

heart

gizzard

feet

Behavioural Adaptations

Birds lay eggs with hard shells. This is because birds' ancestors laid their eggs on land, not in water like some animals. A hard shell was a structural adaptation that prevented the eggs from drying out.

Similarly baby birds hatch with few feathers and are very vulnerable to the cold. Over the generations, the earliest birds adopted the behaviour of caring for their young and keeping them warm, so that their babies would survive. This is an example of a **behavioural adaptation.**

An Australian purple-crowned pigeon sits on her eggs to keep them warm.

A grey fantail feeds its chicks.

ostrich

canary

eagle

Adaptations Help Birds Survive

While all birds have feathers and lay eggs, different kinds of birds look and act differently. A canary looks very different from an ostrich and a toucan looks very different from a Gouldian finch. This is because each **species** has developed **structural** and **behavioral** adaptations that help it survive in a particular habitat. Let's look at some of the specific ways birds have adapted to their habitats.

Gouldian finch

thrush

black swan

toucan

Birds in Motion

All birds have feathered wings, but their wings come in many different shapes and sizes. Birds' wings are adapted for the type of flying they do.

Birds That Fly

Birds that spend most of their time flying often have narrow wings that curve back. Narrow, curved wings give more lift so it takes less energy for these birds to stay in the air. Birds that fly short distances have broad, round wings. These wings are better for quick turns and short bursts of speed.

A swift has narrow, curved wings. It rarely touches land except to roost or nest.

Feather types

Down feathers act as insulation.

Body feathers are sometimes used for display, but are mainly used for protection and added insulation.

Tail feathers are used for steering, balance or display.

Wing feathers make flight possible.

13

Lifting into the air, hovering or staying in one place in the air requires rapid flapping. It takes a lot of energy, so few birds hover. Hummingbirds are very light and have special wing joints that make hovering possible. Other birds, like kestrels, hover briefly and use the wind to help.

Many birds have developed ways of flying that use less energy than flapping, and their wings show it. Gulls, for example, have long, slender wings that allow them to glide. Vultures' broad wings use the lift of warm air to carry them up and up with only a few flaps.

Kestrels hover in the air to watch their prey.

A royal albatross has long, narrow wings that allow it to glide over the ocean for many kilometres.

Birds That Don't Fly

Some birds can't fly because they don't need to. Their ancestors could fly, but over time their **descendants** lost the ability.

Penguins don't fly because they live in a habitat where flying doesn't help them survive. Their food is underwater. They need to dive instead. Their wings propel them through the water after fish.

Australia's largest native bird is the Emu. It is the second largest flightless bird in the world. It grows up to 1.5 metres tall. Its back is decorated with soft, brownish-grey feathers and it has long, powerful legs. Each large foot has three toes.

Ostriches, rheas and cassowaries are too heavy to fly. Flightless birds depend on their legs instead of wings. They run from danger and use their powerful legs to kick when cornered.

Flightless kiwis have adapted to life on the islands of New Zealand. Since the islands have few **predators**, kiwis don't need to fly.

King penguins are well-adapted to their habitat. They have flipper-like wings to propel them through the water.

Bird Legs

All birds have two legs, whether the birds are high-flying or land-loving by nature. However, different **species** have very different types of legs. A roadrunner's legs look very different from the legs of a hummingbird. Differences between each species are **adaptations** to a particular environment.

Birds run, walk and hop. Some climb trees, gripping the bark with their toes. Many water birds, such as ducks, use their broad feet to paddle and steer. Swifts have small legs because they spend most of their lives in the air and rarely need to land.

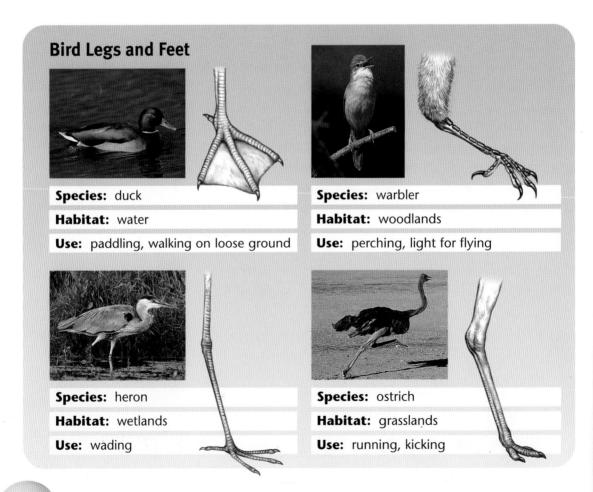

Bird Legs and Feet

Species: duck
Habitat: water
Use: paddling, walking on loose ground

Species: warbler
Habitat: woodlands
Use: perching, light for flying

Species: heron
Habitat: wetlands
Use: wading

Species: ostrich
Habitat: grasslands
Use: running, kicking

Finding Food

The African secretary bird feeds on snakes. It uses its strong feet to trample on its prey, then hurls its victim to the ground to stun it.

Every bird has to eat. Some eat plants. Others live on animals, including insects and fish. A few eat carrion, which is the flesh of dead animals.

Different species eat different types of food. Different habitats offer different food sources. Birds have adapted to find enough food in their environment to survive.

Birds have adapted to their environments in both their structure and behaviour. **Structural adaptations** for finding and eating food are seen in the shape of bills, legs and feet, and in the way birds use their senses. Birds' digestive systems are also adapted to their food. **Behavioural adaptations**, such as flying in flocks, stalking prey and hunting at night also help birds find food.

Greater flamingos eat tiny brine shrimp in salty environments that few other animals can tolerate.

Different Bills for Different Purposes

Birds use their bills, or beaks, and feet to catch, hold, tear apart, crack open and carry their food. Bird bills come in many shapes and sizes. Each is adapted to the birds' needs. The shape of a bill often gives clues about how a bird eats. A bird that probes for food has a long, slender bill. The woodcock, which probes for earthworms, has a special spot on the end of its bill that senses movement. This helps the bird find worms.

Some bills filter water and food like sieves. A flamingo strains water through slits in its bill, and catches bits of food. Many ducks use their bills in a similar way.

Finches, sparrows and cardinals have short, cone-shaped beaks. These are good for crushing or cracking seeds.

Hawks, eagles and owls have hooked bills. These are good for ripping and tearing flesh, and for eating animals that are too large to swallow whole.

Bird Beaks

Bill: spear

Species: heron

Food: fish

Habitat: wetlands

Bill: sieve

Species: flamingo

Food: algae, insects, shrimp

Habitat: marshes

Fruit eaters, such as parrots, have combination bills. The hook at the end helps them rip into the soft part of the fruit while the broad base of the bill is perfect for cracking open the seeds.

Bill: cracker

Species: finch

Food: seed

Habitat: woodlands

Bill: probe

Species: woodcock

Food: earthworms, invertebrates

Habitat: soft ground

Bill: combination

Species: parrot

Food: fruit and seeds

Habitat: tropics

Bill: hook

Species: vulture

Food: carrion

Habitat: open places

The North American osprey, which lives along the coast, could not hold the fish it catches without having well-adapted feet.

Specialized Feet

Birds also have other **adaptations** for catching and eating food. Most birds of prey have sharp talons, or claws, for grabbing and holding their meals. Ospreys have special **scales** on their feet to stop their slippery fish prey from escaping.

Predator birds use their feet to hold food while they tear it into bits that they can swallow easily. Parrots use their feet in the same way though they eat fruit. They hold the fruit and turn it, making it easier to get at the seeds.

Birds of prey, such as this North African lanner falcon, spot animals from high in the air.

Bird Senses

Birds' senses also help them find food. Good vision is very important to most birds. Birds that fly high searching for prey need especially sharp vision. Some see small objects a couple of kilometres away. Some have eyes that face forwards, making it easier to tell how far away something is.

Adaptations such as these mean that a high-flying bird with slightly better vision would be more successful at catching food than one with poorer vision. Good hunters are more likely to survive and pass on their characteristics. Small changes in each generation have led to the adaptations we see today.

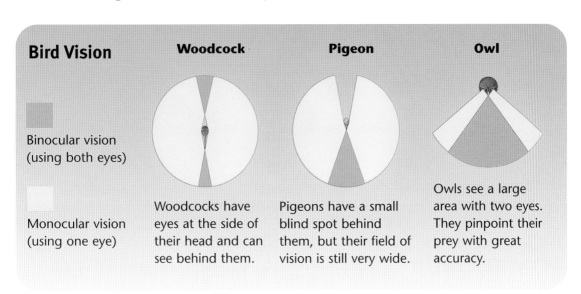

Bird Vision

Woodcock   **Pigeon**   **Owl**

Binocular vision (using both eyes)

Monocular vision (using one eye)

Woodcocks have eyes at the side of their head and can see behind them.

Pigeons have a small blind spot behind them, but their field of vision is still very wide.

Owls see a large area with two eyes. They pinpoint their prey with great accuracy.

Green woodpeckers depend on their hearing to find grubs in trees.

Hearing is more developed in birds that are unable to see their food. Owls that hunt at night can hear mice and track them. Woodpeckers cannot see the insects that crawl beneath the bark of trees, but they can hear them.

Smell is an important sense for a few birds. Turkey vultures eat carrion. They can smell rotting meat even when it is hidden from sight. The kiwi, a **nocturnal** bird, also relies more on smell than sight to find seeds, berries and worms at mealtime.

Taste

Taste doesn't seem to be an important sense to most birds. Birds that eat nectar and fruit do seem to prefer sweet tastes, and a few birds seem to taste salt. However, birds have only a few taste buds far back in their mouths.

Turkey vultures are attracted to the smell of dead animals.

Obtaining Food

Behavioural adaptations also help birds feed successfully. Sometimes the adaptations are social. Many birds fly together in flocks. When one bird finds food, the others share it. Some birds hunt alone, but watch the behaviour of other birds in the area. As soon as one bird finds food, the others join it.

Cattle egrets follow grazing animals.

Cattle egrets often follow grazing animals. The egrets eat insects and small animals that the grazing animals kick up with their feet. Oxpeckers ride on large mammals' backs. They eat ticks and lice that live in the animals' fur.

An African oxpecker has sharp claws that help it to cling to large animals.

Clay-eating macaws

Macaws in the Amazon rainforest eat mostly fruit and seeds, and sometimes clay. Some of these seeds contain poisonous chemicals. Scientists think macaws eat clay because it flushes out these harmful poisons.

Tools That Work

Some birds' eating behaviour involves tools. Gulls carry shellfish high in the air, then drop them onto rocks to crack them open. Some herons drop bits of feathers into the water as bait. When a fish comes to investigate, the heron snaps it up.

Shrikes use tools, too. They catch insects, worms and small animals, including other birds. Then they pin their prey to twigs, thorns or barbed wire to stop them from escaping.

Birds need a great deal of food to live and to fly. Every bird that exists today is adapted to get the food it needs. If a **species** is no longer able to find enough food, it will die out. This is one of the reasons why a species becomes extinct.

A New Caledonian crow uses a stick to dislodge a grub from a tree.

Adaptations Help Birds Stay Safe

The world is a dangerous place for birds. Weather conditions can be harsh and birds can become a meal for another animal. Birds have many features that help protect them from dangers in their habitats.

An Australian pelican cools off by fluttering its large throat pouch.

Maintaining the Right Temperature

All birds are warm-blooded. This means their body temperature stays about the same whatever the weather. As a result, their muscles work well in a wide range of temperatures.

However, it takes special **adaptations**, for warm-blooded animals to remain at the right temperature. If they get too hot, they have to cool down. They dip in water or find a shady spot. They pant. Some birds, such as the Australian pelican, flutter their throats like a built-in fan.

An African Marabou stork keeps itself cool by excreting down its legs.

25

Feathers provide excellent **insulation** in cold weather, helping birds stay warm. Birds make feathers work even better by fluffing them out and trapping pockets of air. Birds shiver, too. This warms them, but it takes up a lot of energy.

Many birds migrate to warmer places when the weather grows cooler. Migration takes a huge amount of energy, and not all birds survive the trip. Overall, the ability to migrate helps **species** survive. Since colder weather usually means fewer sources of food, a migratory bird increases its chances of finding food by flying to a warmer place.

A robin fluffs out its feathers to stay warm in cold weather.

The Arctic tern migrates further than any other bird. Each year it flies from the Arctic to Antarctica and back again.

Avoiding Predators

Staying safe also means avoiding **predators**. Flying is a huge advantage. Some birds' feathers, or **plumage**, also help in another way. They camouflage, or hide, the birds. The colour and patterns of their feathers have evolved to blend in with the surroundings. These birds are difficult for hunters and predators to see when they are still and silent because they blend in so well.

Some birds, such as the ptarmigan, are camouflaged no matter what the season. In the summer, their brown feathers help them disappear into their surroundings. Each autumn, they lose their brown feathers. These are replaced by white feathers which are hard to see against a snowy, winter background.

The American woodcock, with its brown feathers, blends in with the woodland floor.

The willow ptarmigan has pure white plumage in winter and brown plumage in the summer.

27

Keeping Clean

Feathers must be well cared for to keep them in good working order. Birds have developed different behaviours to keep feathers healthy. One way is by bathing. Birds bathe in different ways because different habitats have different conditions and pests. They use water, dust and even ants to help keep their feathers and skin clean.

Birds also **preen**. They fluff their feathers, then clean and comb them with their bills and sometimes their feet. Some birds preen each other.

Like many birds, the chestnut-eared aracari uses its bill to clean and straighten its feathers.

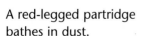

A red-legged partridge bathes in dust.

A northern gannet molts one feather at a time on each wing to remain balanced.

When birds preen, they rub their bills over an oil gland, then coat their feathers with oil. This helps keep feathers from drying out. Ducks and many other water birds have large oil glands to help keep their feathers waterproof.

In spite of care, feathers wear out and have to be replaced in a process called molting. Many birds shed feathers and replace them at certain times of the year, often spring and autumn. The pattern of molting depends on each bird **species**.

The blue-eyed cormorant oils its under-feathers and air-dries its wings.

Adapting and Reproducing

For a bird **species** to continue to exist, it has to reproduce successfully. Reproduction starts with finding a mate.

Finding a Mate

Many species of birds have adapted techniques to attract their mates. These techniques can come in the form of brightly coloured feathers, elaborate dances and songs or other sounds. Males might have gaudy tail feathers or puffed-out throat pouches to attract females. Some birds even perform flying acrobatics to attract their mates.

A male frigate bird inflates its red throat pouch to attract a mate.

A male crown crane performs a dance to attract a female.

Bright colours and intricate flight patterns attract attention. Only the fittest birds have energy to spare for the bigger and brighter displays. As these birds pass on their characteristics on to later generations, the displays became more and more elaborate.

Birds also use sounds to attract mates. Some sing a variety of songs to attract mates. Instead of singing, other birds drum with their wings or their bills on a display site such as a log.

spreading tail feathers

This male lyrebird sings as he spreads his tail feathers in a display to attract a mate.

Building a Nest

Once they have found their mates, most birds build nests to protect their eggs and young hatchlings from bad weather and **predators**. Nest-building varies in different habitats.

Birds have adapted to use whatever is available for nests. Some make nests out of twigs, branches, moss or mud. Most of these nests are well camouflaged. Other birds make nests in muddy banks, hollow trees or even in buildings.

Many seabirds breed in large colonies with only a few pebbles marking a nest. These birds need to be near their food source, but the shoreline habitat has little nesting material. Penguins use their feet to hold their eggs away from the cold.

This jabiru, or Australian black-necked stork, builds its large nest in trees and feeds in swamps and wetlands.

Black guillemots nest in colonies along the coasts of the north Atlantic Ocean.

This reed warbler weaves an intricate nest around reed stems.

Well-Adapted Eggs

Nest **adaptations** protect the birds, their eggs and their young. Eggs come in many shapes and sizes. Many eggs have colours and patterns that blend well with their surroundings. Sandpipers, plovers and other birds that lay their eggs in nests on the ground have eggs that blend in with grass or small stones. Birds that lay eggs in dark holes have less need for camouflage. Their eggs are often white.

Where an egg is laid is determined by its shape. An owl's eggs rest safely inside trees so they tend to be oval in shape. A guillemot's eggs sit on narrow cliff ledges. These eggs are pear-shaped so they won't roll off.

cuckoo's egg

plover's egg

owl's egg

guillemot's egg

ostrich's egg

33

Blackcap warblers are born without feathers and with sealed eyelids.

Raising Young Birds

Every bird **species** alive today has developed successful ways to raise its young. Some chicks have feathers when they hatch. Within hours of hatching, they can leave the nest. They may wander from their family, but they use calls to keep in touch.

Some hatchlings are born without feathers and need complete care. Usually both parents work together to care for them. They feed the baby birds, keep them warm, keep their nest clean and protect them from **predators** until they can care for themselves.

Newly hatched common quail chicks born in Europe, Africa and Eastern Asia are ready to leave the nest – but still need care.

Some birds cooperate to attack any intruder that might threaten their young. This behaviour is called mobbing. They fly at the predator, chase it and even dive-bomb it, to push it away from a nesting area.

Other birds, especially ground-nesters, pretend they are injured when threatened. A parent will lead a predator away from its young by hobbling as if it has a broken wing, so the predator will follow the parent, thinking it is easy prey. Once the predator is far from the nest, the bird flies out of its reach and back to its young.

A mother mallard duck wards off an attack on her chicks from an avocet.

Endangered Birds

Even **species** that are well-adapted to their environments sometimes do not survive. As the number of a species becomes lower, it is regarded as **endangered**. Scientists estimate that more than 90 per cent of all bird species ever in existence have vanished from the Earth. One reason for this is the competitions for resources, such as food and nesting spots. Another reason is that environments change.

Common starlings are found in Australia, Asia, northern Africa, Europe and North America.

Starlings are native to Europe and Asia, but have been introduced almost worldwide. They are now one of the most common birds on many continents. Starlings nest in cavities, or holes. Other cavity-nesting birds, such as bluebirds and red-headed woodpeckers, have to compete with them for living space. Starlings are aggressive so they usually win the fight.

Habitat and Environmental Changes

Any change in habitat conditions can affect a species. A few dry seasons, or drought, can change the vegetation of an area. If some plants die then birds that eat their seeds might not find enough food to survive. On the other hand, birds that eat seeds from plants that grow well in dry conditions might thrive.

Birds that do well under many conditions and eat many different types of food will survive environmental changes more easily than birds with very particular needs.

Cocos Islands finch

large ground finch

medium ground finch

medium tree finch

warbler finch

The bill of each of these finches found in the Galápagos and Cocos Islands is adapted for a particular type of seed.

Dodos died out because they couldn't evolve quickly enough to survive humans who killed them for food.

The Human Factor

As people cut down or burn forests, fill in wetlands and build cities, many habitats are being destroyed. The **species** that depend on those habitats suffer.

Humans are also wily **predators**. In the past, humans have killed off whole species of birds for food and feathers. Their pets kill many birds today.

People benefit in many ways when they save birds from extinction. Birds have provided food for humans for thousands of years. Bird-watching is a hobby for some, but others watch birds for warnings about the health of the environment. A declining bird population can warn humans of possible harm in the environment. It makes sense to help save the birds.

We learn about the environment from birds.

Glossary

adaptations changes that occur in the structures or behaviours of a species over generations that make it easier for the species to survive in its environment

behavioural adaptation an inherited behaviour that makes it easier for a living creature to survive in its habitat

descendants those that will be born to a certain family or group

endangered having such a small population it may become extinct

hypothesize develop an explanation of how or why something happens

insulation material that keeps heat from passing through easily

natural selection the idea that those individuals best adapted to an environment will be the ones most likely to survive

nocturnal active in the night

plumage a bird's feathers

predators animals that capture and eat other animals

preen to clean and comb feathers

scales thin, flat, hard plates forming a layer that covers the skin of certain animals including reptiles and fish

species a class of living things that have the same characteristics and ability to reproduce among themselves such as barn owls

structural adaptations inherited physical forms that make it easier for a living thing to survive in its habitat

Index